First published 1994

ISBN 0 7110 2244 5

© Ian Allan Ltd 1994

Designed by Alan C. Butcher

Published by Ian Allan Publishing

an imprint of Ian Allan Ltd, Terminal House, Station
Approach, Shepperton, Surrey TW17 8AS; and
printed by Ian Allan Printing Ltd Coombelands
House, Coombelands Lane, Addlestone, Weybridge,
Surrey KT15 1HY.

On Great Central Lines

Robert Robotham

Front cover:
'9F' No 92067 emerges into the evening
sunshine from Catesby Tunnel with an up
freight on 10 September 1961. Note the
smoke in the tunnel caused by the up
'runners' as they stormed towards
Woodford Halse.
Colour-Rail

Rear cover:
'O4/8' class 2-8-0 No 63893 heads a
westbound freight past Vale House in
1955.
Colour-Rail

Introduction

On Great Central Lines looks at former Great Central routes in the latter years of steam operation in this country — what many would say were the best years of steam. This book covers the routes from the North West over to Immingham — the old Manchester, Sheffield & Lincoln (MS&L) Railway, plus the London extension of the Great Central Railway, a name first adopted in 1897.

The Great Central was the brain-child of a brilliant business man, Sir Edward Watkin, son of a Manchester cotton baron, who became a railway king. Gradually taking over a collection of northern companies to form the MS&L, plus the Metropolitan and South Eastern, he set upon an extension to London, built to continental loading gauge and opened in 1899 especially for his proposed Channel Tunnel. However, Watkin's dream of Manchester to Paris was never realised for a variety of reasons. Space does not permit those stories to be told here, but George Dow's classic trilogy 'Great Central', which does, is a must for all serious Great Central students.

The building of the GC London extension intensely annoyed the Midland and the London & North Western. To compete with them, the GC had to run the best services with high quality comfort and fast speeds. The GC really became the first marketing led railway employing its own travel agents and 'Rapid Travel In Luxury' slogan. With the brilliant Sir Sam Fay as General Manager, passenger services were expanded, especially cross country long distance services. The development of the port of Immingham was too, a major benefit to the company.

Following the grouping, as part of the LNER firmly in LMS territory, the acquisition of the GC allowed the parent company access to the cross country/Midlands market for freight and passenger traffic. Preparation of the Woodhead routes for electrification was also made, as well as the introduction of the Annesley to Woodford freight service, later to be wound up to virtual Class 1 status in the early BR era. This inter war period is best examined in the two volumes of *The Great Central in LNER Days*, published by Ian Allan.

Following World War 2 services gradually returned to prewar standards although the 'B17' 'Footballers' were replaced on the London extension by 'B1s'. The 'A3s' were back, many sporting new BR blue livery, but accompanied by the new 'V2s'. Manchester to Marylebone had three through expresses leaving at 08.30, 14.10 and 16.05 accompanied by the 07.40 Sheffield-Marylebone 'Master Cutler' introduced as the route's prime business train. Also a 10.00 Bradford and Sheffield-Marylebone express was named the 'South Yorkshireman'. Down services departed Marylebone at 10.00, 12.15, 15.20, 16.50 'South Yorkshireman' for Bradford and the 18.18 'Master Cutler' for Sheffield. The cross country expresses also continued, expanding to all points of the country in summer months. Wartime speed restrictions were gradually lifted and Leicester and Neasden crews with their repaired 'A3s' put in fine performances. Eventually, the 'A3s' were replaced by the 'V2s' — considered better for the GC as smaller driving wheels allowed a faster start — a typical GC tradition along with 'screeching' stops at stations.

This energetic driving method was born out of the need to run faster and better services than the rival routes, and it continued long into BR days, GC crews still believing their line had to compete with the London Midland Region — the GC being part of the Eastern Region. The pattern of local services and long distance stoppers or 'Ords' continued much unchanged along with the famous Liverpool to Harwich boat train services and the newly electrified Manchester to Sheffield service via Woodhead.

Freight traffic had boomed in the war and despite the inevitable fall back the GC still carried vast quantities of coal and ore from its port of Immingham and the South Yorkshire and Nottinghamshire coalfields as well as long distance fish trains. Inter-regional traffic from the Eastern region was taken to west London and semi-finished steel products ran via the Stratford & Midland Junction route from Woodford to Broom

Title page:
'O4/8' No 63819 of Colwick, in typical work stained condition, rolls through 'the 'Vic' with an up freight. Nottingham Victoria station site was cut into rock and is now a shopping centre and car park. Situated in the centre of Nottingham, unlike the Midland station, it would have been an ideal candidate for a combined station and shopping facility. The date is 11 April 1964 and already the station signs are bearing the maroon of the London Midland Region.
Neville Simms

Above:
The classic GC freights were the Annesley-Woodford express services that ran between the two yards hauled by the famous '9F' class 2-10-0s. In true GC fashion, No 92073 of Annesley is going hard through Rugby Central with an up 'runner' or 'Windcutter' on 28 December 1964.
Neville Simms

junction and the west. The most famous freight workings on the GC were the Annesley-Woodford fast freights known as 'runners' or 'Windcutters' because of their speed. Fine tuned with the introduction of the standard Class 9F 2-10-0s these trains often ran with speeds in the high 60s. Manchester to Sheffield and Wath in the north also saw vast tonnages of freight moved across the Pennines using the 'EM2' electric locomotives or the famous Robinson 'O1s' as well as the LNER Garratt. Many other inter-regional freight and parcel services would run via the Western Region link from Culworth junction to Banbury and there were also overnight mail trains from Manchester and Liverpool to Marylebone and return along with the famous 00.45 'Newspaper' flyer from Marylebone to Nottingham.

Despite this intensity of service, plans were afoot to close the main line, even before the Beeching era. It soon became clear that the route would be transferred to the control of the London Midland Region, which happened in February 1958. The chance to seize control of its long time rival was not welcomed by the Derby and Euston dominated management who were concerned to develop their traditional routes, the Midland and the London & North Western.

Express services were withdrawn on 2 January 1960. Local services continued but the replacement semi-fast service, (08.38, 14.38 and 16.38 from Marylebone to Nottingham and 08.15, 12.25 and 17.15 return), was badly timed to connect with anything north of Nottingham and had no catering facilities. It was no match for competing Midland and West Coast services, and the 'Master Cutler' had been re-routed via Retford to Kings Cross two years previously. A large number of cross country services still ran, (along with diverted sleepers from the West Coast route during electrification), but by 1965 all except the York-Bournemouth had gone. Local services and stations were reduced most closing in May 1963. Eventually the line's main traffic, freight, was transferred away and the Windcutters ceased to run in June 1965.

The last day of the London extension was a sad affair — a more detailed account being available in *The Last Years of The Great Central* published by Ian Allan. Following closure a local DMU service from Nottingham to Rugby lasted only until May 1969. Even the Manchester-Sheffield expresses were withdrawn along with total closure of the electrified system through Woodhead. Demolition men moved in with haste in all areas, many structures being instantly demolished following closures — almost as if it was being made sure that the GC could never come back!

With much of the main GC network closed, most of the original MS&L services found themselves diverted onto Midland lines — notably the Manchester-Harwich boat train and even the Sheffield-Manchester express service was replaced by DMUs on the Hope Valley. Immingham docks are a shadow of their former selves and most surviving GC routes have been severely rationalised and become 'basic railways'. However, where there has been investment, business has increased, evident in the total route modernisation of the GC suburban lines from Marylebone, now known as the Chiltern Line. Most of the coal was transferred to the new 'merry go round' operation and the rest of the traffic either transferred to the other routes or switched to road.

Much debate could be made about the correctness to run down the GC lines. It was not inevitable that the main line should have closed or the Sheffield-Manchester services been withdrawn. They closed mainly because management at the time did not see the Great Central as 'their' railway and in the era of rationalisation and cost cutting the GC routes seem to have lost out in the process.

How premature those decisions were is all too evident now as Watkin's dream of a channel tunnel is realised. It is a sobering thought that the only main line in the United Kingdom capable of taking continental loading gauge stock from the south to the north was closed 28 years ago. That route was the Great Central.

Robert Robotham
Charlbury 1994

Special thanks are due to Ron White and Wendy Chapman.

Marylebone to Nottingham

The 'classic' last years service operated on the GCR main line was three semi-fasts in either direction from Marylebone to Nottingham only, with no catering or useful connections north of Nottingham. They were no match for the expresses they replaced or those operating on the rival Midland route from St Pancras. 'Black 5' No 44572 is shown leaving Marylebone on 2 September 1966, with the last down semi-fast of the day, the 16.38 to Nottingham, one day before closure.
Roy Hobbs

A general view of Marylebone station early one morning in March 1963 shows a Fairburn '4MT' 2-6-4T shunting a variety of vans. In the foreground are the DMU sets used on the Aylesbury and High Wycombe services, (and even one turn to Nottingham at the end!), which had displaced the Stanier and Fairburn locomotives on the Marylebone suburban services. They in turn had replaced the Eastern Region 'L1s' before 'London Midlandisation' took hold.
Roy Hobbs

Left:
'Black 5' No 45450 pauses at Aylesbury with an afternoon down semi-fast on 16 February 1961. After the hard climb over the Chilterns the driver takes the chance to top up the tender tank, before the dash to Brackley Central.
Colour-Rail

Right:
On the GC/GW joint line, Fairburn 2-6-4T No 42090 awaits departure from High Wycombe with a stopping service, the 08.05 Brackley Central-Marylebone on 12 March 1961.
G. T. Robinson

English Electric Type 3 diesel No D6818 heads an up cup final special through Princes Risborough in May 1963. The destination is Wembley Hill and Leicester City fans will be disappointed as their team loses!

The late J. P. Mullett/Colour-Rail (DE504)

Left:
'K3' No 61824 and an unidentified sister pass through Finmere with an evening local from Marylebone to Woodford on 22 March 1961. Not really near any large population, Finmere was originally the GC station for Buckingham. Traditionally the GC ran long distance stopping trains such as this, known to railwaymen as 'Ords'. Double heading was rare on the GC as it was seen as very uneconomic.
F. G. Cockman/Colour-Rail

Right:
The link to the Great Western at Banbury from Culworth junction saw a great deal of inter-regional freight, passenger and parcels traffic. GW locomotives were daily visitors and here, 'Hall' class No 7901 *Doddington Hall* passes through a deep cutting near Thorpe Mandeville with a northbound inter-regional express freight on 12 October 1963.
M. Mensing

Right:
Brackley's fine viaduct over the river Great Ouse is crossed by an afternoon semi-fast from Marylebone to Nottingham with 'Black 5' No 44941 in charge on 28 May 1966. Only four months to go and then only demolition awaited the fine structure.
The late J. P. Mullett/Colour-Rail

Left:
The 12.30 pm 'Banbury Motor' rushes towards Woodford from Banbury on 12 October 1963 hauled by Fairburn 2-6-4T No 42082 from Woodford Shed. This service provided a useful link between the two main lines and platforms at the north end of Banbury station for it still survive today.
M. Mensing

Below:
The 08.38 from Marylebone to Nottingham and the return 12.25 working were turned over from steam to a suburban DMU in the last years of operation. Such 'run down' services seen more recently on the Settle-Carlisle line would today have produced major campaigns for development and line retention, but in the early 1960s this just did not happen. Here the DMU leaves Woodford for Marylebone with the 12.30 from Nottingham Victoria on 3 April 1965. The link to the SMJ route to Broom junction, a heavy freight carrier, is seen through the left hand arch.
M. Mensing

Standard Mogul No 76087 storms away
from Woodford with a local goods trip for
London on a crisp day on 23 February
1963. Services such as this served the local
stations in the immediate area, and indeed
No 76087 was shedded at Woodford.

Neville Simms

Right:
'B1' 4-6-0 No 61249 heads towards Woodford Halse station with an up semi-fast from Nottingham Victoria to Marylebone. At first the semi-fasts were run as long trains with smart point to point timings. However, they gradually became more unattractive and eventually ended up as four coach sets. Some would say this was part of the deliberate run down of the GCR.
10 April 1961.
The late J. P. Mullett/ Colour-Rail

Left:
The extensive yards at Woodford Halse were situated on either side of the main lines. On the up side was the shed — always a cosmopolitan affair due to the number of inter-regional workings. This September 1961 shot shows nine locomotives, ex-LNER, Standard and 'Austerities' being present.
The late J. P. Mullett/ Colour-Rail (BRE321)

Left:
'Jubilee' 4-6-0 No 45598 *Basutoland* of Burton shed takes water on Charwelton troughs with an up all first class cup final special from Leicester Central to Wembley Hill in May 1963. One wonders what BR would make of the watching photographers so close to a main line in 1994!
T. Tomalin/Colour-Rail (BRE1097)

Above:
The last inter-regional passenger service to use the GCR route was the York-Bournemouth, (Newcastle-Poole in summer), and often bought Western Region locomotives to Nottingham. Class 37 locos took over this service from steam, but right at the end Brush Type 4 locomotives, in this case No D1871 of Tinsley, were the usual power. No D1871 storms out of Catesby tunnel with the southbound service on 20 August 1966.
Neville Simms

The 1.15pm Sunday semi-fast service storms away from Rugby Central with standard Class 5 No 73159 in charge on 14 October 1962. Despite being non-LNER, these locos were liked by GC crews much more than the 'old enemy' ex-LMS types.
Neville Simms

Work stained rebuilt 'Jubilee' No 45735 *Comet* passes through Rugby Central with the 11.15 Nottingham-Neasden parcels in March 1964. This train was the return working of the newspaper vans hauled down to Nottingham the night before. The GC newspaper train was a famous service still running to express standards on the GC late on in its life as a through route. *D. Smith/Colour-Rail (BRM685)*

Left:
Another 'runner' storms through Rugby's 'Birdcage' bridge over the West Coast main line, (still standing), with '9F' No 92132 at the head. No speed restrictions here or through the station, unlike the LNWR route below. The date is October 1964.
D. Smith/Colour-Rail (BRE612)

Above:
'9F' No 92013 races through Ashby Magna with a train of wood on 9 May 1964. The freight department were taking no chance hence the van and brake as 'barrier' vehicles.
Barry Hilton

Below:
'V2' No 60963 brings a welcome LNER scene back to the
increasingly Midlandised GC route as it heads the 11.15
Nottingham-Neasden parcels past Leicester South Goods box on
18 April 1964. The residents of the houses behind the locomotive
regularly got their washing blackened by the typical enterprising
departures!
Barry Hilton

Right:
Leicester had its own shed, famous with Neasden for being the
home of the 'A3s' and 'V2s', and produced the eager express
passenger crews for the line. No 76052 is seen on the shed in
August 1962 before working back to the London area. Leicester
shed closed in July 1964 as the run down quickened.
K. C. H. Fairey/Colour-Rail (BRE518)

'Black 5' No 44847 leaves Leicester Central with a bank holiday excursion to London on 6 August 1962. It is seen at Leicester North Goods junction passing the carriage sheds just behind the locomotive.
Geoff King

'9F' No 92010 runs through Leicester Central with an up 'runner' on 31 August 1961. The front of the station is situated just behind the locomotive, platforms being accessed by a subway. Today Leicester Central is an industrial estate. *Colour-Rail*

'Black 5' No 44760 races through Quorn & Woodhouse with the 17.15 Nottingham-Marylebone in June 1966. The semi-fasts were all reduced to four coaches by this time, the exception being this service when the passenger accommodation was strengthened for commuter traffic. (Also it helped return the passenger coaches for the down 'newspaper' from London.)
W. Chapman/Colour-Rail (BRM911)

Below:

Below:
This 1960 shot of Loughborough Central is relatively similar today with the preserved Great Central operating a Loughborough-Leicester North service. Apart from the loss of the goods yard on the left the loop and the main line still exist. Here a '9F' and 'Black 5' are seen, the former leading a northbound freight, the latter shunting coaches. Well worth a visit today!
Main Line Steam Trust

Right:
Early September 1966 sees 'Black 5' 4-6-0 No 44936 at East Leake with the 17.15 up semi-fast from Nottingham to Marylebone. With closure on 3 September for the GC as a through route just days away; enthusiasts take the opportunity for a final trip as they 'window hang' from the leading coach.
Main Line Steam Trust

Below:
'9F' No 92072 races through Ruddington in June 1963 with
another 'runner'. Ruddington was the junction for the MoD depot
and the source of much traffic for the GCR. Now the MoD depot is
the home of the emerging Country Park & Heritage Centre, where
the Great Central (Nottingham) Ltd are based and will eventually
become the northern terminus of the preserved line from Leicester
North.
Main Line Steam Trust

Right:
Following the withdrawal of through passenger services on
3 September 1966, a truncated Nottingham-Rugby service was
introduced, operated by DMUs. Nottingham Victoria was closed in
September 1967 and Arkwright Street station was re-opened as a
rather inconvenient terminus. Here, a DMU awaits departure for
Rugby Central in March 1969.
M. Burnett/Colour-Rail (DE1424)

Left:
'Black 5' No 45301 leaves Nottingham Victoria with an excursion for the east coast in summer 1963. The link to the GN route to Grantham gave the GC access to the lucrative holiday maker traffic most of which today is car-bound.
J. Proctor/Colour-Rail (BRM338)

Below:
'Royal Scot' No 46110 *Grenadier Guardsman* leaves Nottingham Victoria with the 11.15am parcels service for London. These vans originated on the down 'newspaper' that had worked northwards earlier in the day. The scene was recorded in June 1963.
D. H. Ballantyne/Colour-Rail

Left:
'Britannia' No 70054 *Dornoch Firth* blows off inside the cathedral atmosphere of Nottingham Victoria after arriving with the 16.38 from Marylebone in October 1965. High sided tender locomotives were transferred to the GC line as locomotive servicing points were closed and larger mileages were expected between replenishment.
Bill Chapman/Colour-Rail (BRM513)

Above
Through inter-regional services had to change locomotives at Nottingham Victoria after Leicester shed had closed in July 1964. 'Hall' class No 6911 *Holker Hall* has disgraced itself by backing off the turntable at Nottingham Victoria — no doubt much to the amusement of GC line crews who had a disregard for anything Great Western, which was nicknamed the 'Gas Works Railway'. August 1964. *B. Timmins/Colour-Rail (BRW770)*

Right:
English Electric Type 3, (now Class 37) No D6810 heads the 10.30 Poole-York north of Bulwell Common with the maroon stock provided by the London Midland Region for the service. The other set came from the Southern and was therefore green. May 1966 was only five months from closure and near to conversion of this service to Class 47 haulage.
W. Chapman/ Colour-Rail (DE597)

Right:
Class D11/1 'Large Director' of 1920 vintage No 62670 *Marne* passes through Hucknall Central with an 'Ord' for Nottingham on 8 December 1957. The GC 'Directors' were very successful strong locomotives and lasted well into the final years of the London Extension.
Colour-Rail

Left:
The other named GCR express was the 'South Yorkshireman' from Bradford to Marylebone and return. Here 'B1' No 61380 races south near Tibshelf with the up service in September 1959. Locomotives would be changed at Leicester Central in both directions.
M. Mensing/Colour-Rail (BRE348)

Below:
Class K3 2-6-0 No 61974 is seen in the deep cutting south of Heath station with the 10.09am Sheffield Victoria-Nottinghan Victoria 'Ord' on 29 September 1959.
M. Mensing.

Chesterfield's crooked church spire over looks 'O1' No 63897 climbing away from the town with an up freight in June 1962. The station was a low level affair and the route was situated on a loop from junctions off the main line at Staveley Town South and Heath.

Colour-Rail (BRE32)

Class D11/1 No 62660 *Butler Henderson* leaves Killamarsh Central with an up 'Ord' in September 1960. Thankfully the locomotive now resides in the National Railway Museum after a long spell working at Loughborough on the preserved Great Central to Leicester North. Will it return in 1999 for the centenary of the London extension? *Colour-Rail (BRE10)*

Left:
'B1' No 61182 stands in Sheffield Victoria having just backed onto an up express for Marylebone in March 1954. On a Manchester-Marylebone service locomotives were changed at Sheffield and Leicester.
J. Davenport/ Colour-Rail (BRE345)

Right
'B1' No 61127 stands in Sheffield Victoria with station pilot headlamps fixed. Sheffield Victoria looks quite modern with overhead wires and in 1954 was still a centre for expresses to Manchester, Liverpool, the northeast, the southwest, London and the Eastern Counties — little remains today.
The late W. Oliver/ Colour-Rail

Left:
No E27000 *Electra* is seen before naming outside Sheffield
Victoria. It seems amazing that a fully modernised electrified
route between Sheffield and Manchester was abandoned in favour
of another route in the 1970s. This scene was glimpsed in
September 1958.
G. Devine/Colour-Rail (DE535)

Below:
English Electric Type 3 No D6743 waits at Sheffield Victoria with
the overnight mail from Sheffield to Swindon. This became a
regular diesel turn in the latter years of the route. The date is April
1966.
G. Warnes/Colour-Rail (DE1034)

3 September 1966
The Last Day of the London Extension

Left:
'Black 5' No 45292 heads south with the last 11.15 Nottingham-Neasden parcels. Chalked on the smoke box door is 'The Last Day — Great Central'. Quainton Road looks much the same as it always has, track still being extant in the Brill branch platform on the left.
Colour-Rail

Below:
'Black 5' No 44872 had worked the 08.15 from Nottingham to Marylebone and was diagrammed to return on the 14.38 down. However, she failed at Aylesbury being replaced by No D5089. No D5000 worked the train back to Nottingham. Here she is passing Charwelton's demolished station with the last 14.38.
M. Mensing

Below:
No 44984 worked the last up 17.15 semi-fast ex-Nottingham and, complete with wreath, races through Whetstone. No 44984 then worked the last Marylebone-Manchester mail which left at 22.45, thus being the last steam locomotive to work a GC main line train out of Marylebone.
Barry Hilton

Right:
A Waterloo-Nottingham railtour complete with 'Merchant Navy' class pacific No 35030 *Elder Dempster Lines* is seen arriving at Nottingham Victoria. The 'Great Central Railtour' also toured the northern part of the route hauled by two 'B1s'.
John Wade

'B1s' Nos 61173 and 61131 are seen
passing Bagthorpe junction on their way
back to Nottingham with the 'Great
Central Railtour'. The GC was no stranger

to green coaches — the Bournemouth-
York express being formed of one set of
green from the Southern Region.
W. Chapman/Colour-Rail (BRE344)

Wandering Around Woodhead

'EM1' No 27004 *Juno* is seen passing
Penistone on a Manchester London Road-
Sheffield Victoria express in August 1965.

The locomotive is carrying early BR blue
livery before the days of yellow warning
panels. *C. A. Davies/Colour-Rail (DE861)*

Below:
'K3' No 61913 is seen leaving Hadfield with excursion stock on
4 May 1957. These locomotives were very powerful for their size
and were good performers on the GC routes.
The late W. Oliver/Colour-Rail

Right:
An immaculate 'B1', No 61188, meets horsepower of another
kind at Dinting whilst on an engineers' train in 1963.
Colour-Rail

Below:
'EM1' No 26028 enters Dinting with an eastbound freight train, showing a fine view of the viaduct. The viaduct had to be strengthened following its building and between the main piers can be seen new supports. The date is April 1966.
B. Magilton/Colour-Rail (DE955)

Right:
A Class 506 EMU in original green livery is seen at Dinting station with a Manchester London Road (now re-named Piccadilly) service in August 1954.
The late W. Oliver/Colour-Rail (DE932)

Above:
'O4/6' No 63588 runs through Mottram Yard with a train of tipplers in 1953. Quite often on the Woodhead route steam and electric locomotives would double up either for more power or to provide a balancing working.
The late W. Oliver/Colour-Rail

Right:
The industrial northwest is shown to good effect as Robinson 'O4/3' No 63870 races through Hyde junction with another long freight service in 1952.
The late W. Oliver/Colour-Rail (BRE743)

Right:
Also seen at Hyde junction is 'C13' 4-4-2T No 67438 propelling two GC teak coaches. The 'C13s' were first built in 1903 at Gorton and lasted well into BR days — in this case 1952.
The late W. Oliver/Colour-Rail (BRE711)

Far right:
No E26000 *Tommy* runs through Guide Bridge light engine in September 1966. The name *Tommy* was given to the locomotive by Dutch railwaymen to whom it was on loan from 30 August 1947 to 1952. The naming ceremony was on 30 June 1952.
B. Magilton/Colour -Rail

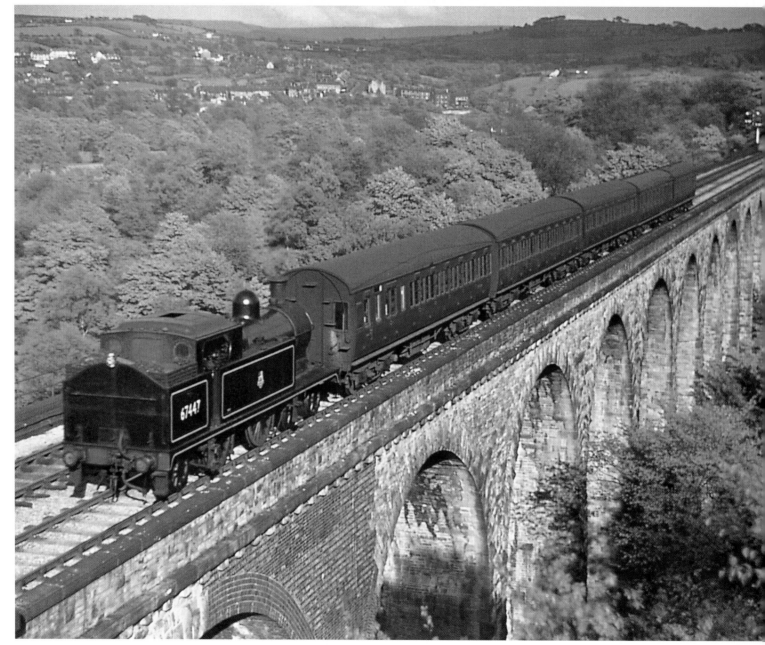

Manchester Suburban

Left:
A Class C14, No 67447, in ex-works condition is seen bunker first on Marple viaduct with an up local for Hayfield in 1953.
E. Oldham/Colour-Rail (BRE111)

Above:
Another 'C14' No 67448 is seen at Birch Vale with a local service on the Hayfield-Marple line on 30 April 1957. As well as its own routes in the Manchester area, the GC had formed an alliance with the Midland and the Great Northern which was called the 'Cheshire Lines Committee'. Romily, Hayfield and Marple were all part of the CLC which extended over to Liverpool and Chester and gave the GC access to Manchester Central as well as London Road.
The late W. Oliver/Colour-Rail

Left:
'Director' Class D10 No 62656 *Sir Clement Royds* is seen on the turntable at Manchester Central in 1952, with a 'B1' behind. The 'Directors' were often used on the expresses to Liverpool and over into Cheshire, being renowned for fine turns of speed.
The late W. Oliver/Colour-Rail (BRE372)

Below:
Fowler 2-6-4T No 42372 leaves Chester Northgate with the 16.53 to Wrexham Central on 27 August 1959. Chester Northgate was the Cheshire Lines terminus from Manchester and a variety of other routes, notably the line to Birkenhead and Wrexham.
G. H. Hunt/Colour-Rail

On Shed

Above:
The GC even penetrated as far as Wrexham after it had taken over the Wrexham, Mold & Connor's Quay Railway in 1905. The shed was called Wrexham Rhosddu and locomotive Nos 68565, 69346, 40084 and 84000 are seen amongst others on duty. The date is 1957.
A. Sainty/Colour-Rail (BRE755)

Right:
'O4/3' No 63701 stands at Langwith junction locomotive shed in June 1965. This locomotive was the last one to remain in service with an original Belpaire firebox. Langwith was on the GC route through The Dukeries, that ran from Lincoln to Chesterfield, (the old Lincolnshire, Derbyshire & East Coast line), with spurs off to Mansfield and Killamarsh. The line is in the heart of the Nottinghamshire coalfield and Langwith Junction provided the motive power for the vast number of coal services.
J. B. Snell/Colour-Rail

Left:
A trio of locomotives, Nos 63986, 63586 and 63954, run through Worksop on the GC route from Sheffield to Lincoln in August 1961. No 63986 is Class 02, No 63586 an 'O4/1' and No 63954 another 'O2'.
F. G. Cockman/Colour-Rail (BRE742)

Right:
GC 'Director' Class D11/1 No 62660 *Butler Henderson* is seen bringing a Cleethorpes-Manchester train around the old sharp curve into Retford station in July 1959.
T. B. Owen/Colour-Rail (BRE712)

Right:
'O4/1' No 63632 and an unidentified 'Austerity' reverse over the GN main line on the flat crossing at Retford in July 1963. Always a bottle-neck, the problem of the flat crossing was cured by the construction of a fly under and low level station that is still used today. The station can be glimpsed behind the two locomotives.
Colour-Rail

Below:
'Austerity' 2-8-0 No 90384 runs into Lincoln Central over the
river Witham with another freight for Barnetby and Immingham in
June 1960. Lincoln Cathedral, a landmark for RAF bomber crews
in the war, dominates the scene.
J. M. Bairstow/Colour-Rail (BRE904)

Right:
On the GC route from Penistone to Doncaster the line passed
through Barnsley. Here a good view of the shed is seen with many
locomotives, Nos 64902 and 63697 in the foreground, on a sunny
day in August 1959.
G. Warnes/Colour-Rail (BRE521)

Left:
Left:
'O4/8' No 63899 is seen at Elsecar junction on a heavy freight train on 23 March 1960. The wires are up at this point for the freights from Wath yard that took the Woodhead route over the Pennines.
The late J. P. Mullett/Colour-Rail

Below:
Class J11/3 0-6-0 No 64393 and a host of other GC types stand at Mexborough shed in August 1959. Mexborough was an important junction for the three routes from Wath, Sheffield and Doncaster which come together there.
Colour-Rail (BRE465)

Above:
'O4/8' No 63785 storms over the frozen canal at Thorne with a freight in January 1963. Thorne is on the Doncaster-Barnetby route which passes through the important steel producing area of Scunthorpe and Frodingham.
G. Warnes/Colour-Rail (BRE510)

Right:
On a typical bleak Frodingham day 'O1' 2-8-0 No 63589 stands on shed awaiting its next turn of duty.
Colour-Rail

'K2' 2-6-0 No 61742 runs through
Barnetby with a heavy freight in 1958.
Barnetby in the 1990s is not as busy as it
used to be, but it is still the junction of
three GC routes from Cleethorpes to
Doncaster, Gainsborough/Sheffield and
Lincoln.
Colour-Rail

Left:
Grimsby & Immingham car No 14 in BR green is seen at Immingham dock in July 1956. Opened in 1912 the electric tramway ran from Grimsby to Immingham with a repair depot at Pyewipe.
T. J. Edgington/Colour-Rail (DE496)

Above
'B1' 4-6-0 No 61250 *A. Harold Bibby* passes over Cleethorpe Road Crossing in Grimsby with empty coaching stock in June 1964.
G. Devine/Colour-Rail (BRE859)

Left:
'Britannia' class 4-6-2 No 70012 *John O' Gaunt* is seen at Cleethorpes with an RCTS special in 1965. Some 'Britannias' were allocated to Immingham shed and worked the famous fish trains to the south along the London extension and on to Swindon.
Main Line Steam Trust

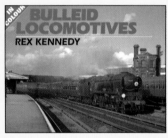